IPAD PRO USER GUIDE

(2022)

Detailed Instructions with Illustrations on How to Setup and Use the iPad Pro 11-inch & 12.9-inch (M2 chip & iPadOS 16 Manual) With Tip and Tricks for Beginners and Senior

SCOTT WHETZEL

Table of Contents

ABOUT THE BOOK

How can you operate, use, and set up your new iPad Pro 11-inch & 12.9-inch like an expert?

These new tablets (iPad Pro 11-inch & 12.9-inch), which are at the center of an ever-expanding collection of gadgets that also includes an apple pencil, magic keyboard, and headphones, are powered by the next-generation M2 chip processor and pre-installed with iPados 16. These are all equipped with the sophisticated hardware you would anticipate from apple, and they work perfectly to benefit apple tablet users.

Using this book as a guide, you may navigate the 36 chapters explaining how users will setups, use, install, configure, take pictures, cameras, and videos, use stage manager, apple pencil, magic keyboard, unlock, boot device, and lots more for novice and masters as it is explained in a step by step manner with illustrations, and icons for easy readers understanding

Introduction

The new iPad Pro is an intriguing gadget because of its sophisticated appearance and potent new M2 CPU, it stands out among other tablets as one of the best.
 Stage Manager and Apple Pencil now perfectly work in this new device, two new iPadOS 16 features, perform admirably on the tablet.

Through the Apple online store, you will be able to acquire the brand-new iPad Pro 2022. The 12.9-inch iPad Pro costs $1,099/£1,249/AU$1,399, while the 11-inch model is currently $799/£899/AU$1,399 in price.

If you prefer the Wi-Fi + Cellular, the 11-inch version can be purchased at $999/£899/AU$1,399 as a starting price. beginning at $1,299, £1,429, or AU The 12-inch Wi-Fi + Cellular version can be purchased at $2,149.

Design

- The 2022 new gadget shares the identical blueprint as the previous gadgets such as the iPad Pro 2020 & 2021. Though its aluminum frame and tiny bezels continue to be eye-catching.
- The magnitude of the m2 iPad 2022 are 11.04 x 8.46 x 0.25 inches, and it has the same weight of 1.5 pounds as the model from the previous year. The weight is increased by the Magic Keyboard to 3 pounds, which is slightly more than the 2.7 pounds each of the MacBook Air 2022 and Dell XPS 13 OLED 2022.
- The light weight of the tablet makes it comfortable to carry for extended periods even without the keyboard connection. The iPad Pro, in contrast to the enormous 14-inch

Galaxy Tab Ultra, isn't overly large and is comfortable in hands.
- As far as buttons and ports are talked about, nothing has been modified. When holding the iPad vertically, like a sheet of paper, there are 2 volume knobs/buttons on the rightward flank.

Display

- This new gadget had a sizable 12.9-inch mini-LED display with 2,732 x 2,048-pixel resolution and a refresh rate of up to 120Hz.
- Similar to the iPad Pro 2021, the new iPad Pro's XDR screen creates its 1,000,000:1 contrast ratio using local dimming zones.

Performance and 5G

The company's M2 chip is included in the iPad gadget. Therefore, it shouldn't be surprising that the novel tablet functions better than the old one.

- This is the latest top-tier device if you enjoy playing games on an iPad.
- Cameras are the same as on the iPad Pro 2021, and Center Stage is still an excellent feature.
- The cameras on the new iPad Pro are identical to those on the model from a year ago.
- Although I'll never support using a tablet to take selfies, if you're tempted to do so, this is also accurate when participating in video conferences with coworkers, friends, or family. The back's 12MP camera likewise produces high-quality images.

Software

Stage Manager is pre-installed in iPadOS 16 and performs nicely on the huge iPad Pro screen.

- Your open apps will be consigned to a pile of tiles on the flank of the display or screen as Stage Manager moves anything you're running or operating into the middle of your display. Because the tiles are so little, you will be able to focus on what is be done while keeping an eye on everything else.
- Apple Pencil Hover, which is only available on the iPad Pro 2022 with an M2-powered tablet, is the second significant innovation. The iPad Pro allows you to preview your mark before you make it and will be able to sense the Pencil close to 12 mm over the display screen.

Apple Pencil 2 and Magic Keyboard

Optional accessories are useful but pricey.

My two favorite accessories are the Apple Magic Keyboard ($349 USD) and the Apple Pencil 2 ($129 USD). While the latter enables you to write or draw on the tablet, the former delivers capability comparable to that of the iPad Pro laptop.

No matter how forcefully you type, the tablet is kept in place by the Magic Keyboard's robust base. You can obtain the ideal viewing angle thanks to the floating design.

CHAPTER 1

Boot/ Turn on iPad

1. Click & swiftly free the up volume button

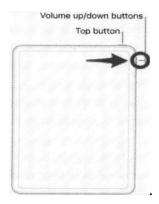

2. Click & swiftly free the down volume button

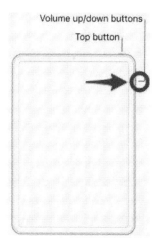

3. Holddown the button at the upper section til the company logo pop-up, then free the knob

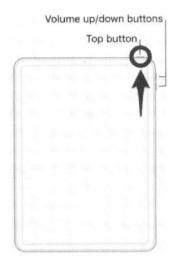

IPad Rebooting

1. Click & holddown the button at the upper or flank side til the slider pop-up.

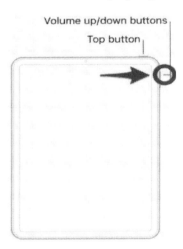

2. Pull the slider to toggle off.

3. Pause for some seconds, then click the button at the upper or flank side again til the phones company logo pop-up; Your gadget will reboot.

Waking up iPad

You can use one of the following to awaken the iPad:

1. Click the top button first.
2. Tap the display.

Installing/removing a SIM card

It is possible to install either an SIM card or a SIM make available by a carrier.

1. To eject the SIM tray, push in toward the iPad when placing a paper snip or SIM expel tool (not supplied) into the hole in the SIM tray.

Note: Depending on the device version & your state or region, the SIM tray may be shaped differently or oriented.

Take the iPad's tray out.

1. Put the SIM in the tray in step 1(The right alignment is determined by the angled corner)
2. Reinstall the tray on the iPad
3. Carefully input the PIN if you've prior setting one up on the SIM.

Install the SIM card

1. In the tiny slot on the SIM card dish, slot in a paper snip or the SIM eject tool (which is not included).

2. To eject the sim plate, slot in the direction of the iPad.
3. Take the iPad's tray out.
4. Put the SIM in the tray in step 4. The correct direction is determined by the angular angle.
5. Put the tray back into the iPad.
6. If a PIN has been previously set on the SIM card, carefully enter it when required.

Charge your gadget's battery

Any of the subsequent can be done to recharge your iPad's battery:

1. Utilizing the cord and power adapter, plug the iPad into a power outlet. (View the iPad's included accessories when you purchase your device)

Note: An iPad must have a power source to begin an iCloud backup or cellular PC syncing.

2. Use a cable to link your iPad gadget to computer
3. You can connect an iPad to a laptop PC directly using a USB connection or adapter.
4. Attach the iPad to your Pc's USB port utilizing the charging wire that came with it.
5. Try any of the subsequent if the cable and computer port are incompatible:
   - Use a USB-C to USB adapter with a USB-A cable if your laptop/Pc has a USB port and your iPad arrived with a

USB-C charging cable (each sold separately).
- (Thunderbolt devices like the 12.9-inch (5th generation) & 11-inch (3rd generation) can be connected using Thunderbolt or USB cords.)
6. Execute any of the subsequent:
    - Initialize your iPad configuration.
    - Add an iPad to your Mac as another display.
    - Share folders via your computer and iPad.
    - Syncing content between your computer and iPad.
    - Using the Wi-Fi + Cellular versions of your iPad to connect it to your computer.
    - Delete all of the iPad's data and configurations using your computer.
    - Utilizing your computer, update your iPad.

Show iPad Battery Percentage

Make a battery widget available on your home screen.

1. Click & holddown the home screen's wallpaper pending when the applications starts vibrating.
2. Tap Batteries after tapping the Add Device button at the upper edge of the display.
3. To view size options, slide leftward & rightward on the battery icon widgets. (Different sizes display information in different ways.)
4. When the desired size appears, select Add Tool, then select Done

CHAPTER 2

Activate and configure your iPad

Activate and configure your iPad

1. Press & hold-down the upper knob or button pending when you see the Apple symbol.
2. It's possible that the battery needs charging if the iPad won't turn on.

Do the following:

- Trail the setup steps displayed on screen after selecting Setup Manually.

Switching from your Android gadget to an iPad

Perform the following on an iPad:

1. Go through the setup wizard.
2. Via the Applications & Data display screen, select the Transfer data from Android button.

Do the following on your Android phone or tablet:

1. Switch on Wi-Fi first.
2. Launch the iOS Move to the app.
3. Comply with the on-screen instructions.

Configure cellular service on an iPad with Wi-Fi + Cellular

Set up your cellular plan with eSIM.

1. Select Cellular Data under Settings.
2. Choose one of these options:
   - Choose a carrier, then adhere to the onscreen steps to configure your iPad's initial cellular plan.
   - To include a new cellular plan to your iPad, choose Install another Plan.
   - For Barcode scanning, tap Other that your carrier has provided. Place the iPad in a frame with the Barcode that your carrier provided, or enter the information manually. Your carrier might request that you input a confirmation code.

Setting your mobile plan up via SIM card or an inbuilt Apple SIM

1. Select Cellular Data under Settings.
2. Choose include a different Plan, then adhere to the on-screen prompts. You will be able to either pick a carrier & a plan, or you will be able to include your iPad to a accessible plan.

Resetting iPad to factory setup

For you to restore all your settings the way you prefer, which may take some time. In resetting your iPad to factory settings:

1. Launch the Settings application
2. Toggle to Genera
3. Click Transfer or Reset iPad.

4. Press Reset.

CHAPTER 3

Making Connections on your iPad 2022

Link your device to the internet

Set up a Wi-Fi network on your iPad.

1. Open Settings > Wi-Fi and activate Wi-Fi.
2. Click any of the subsequent:
   - A network: Whenever prompted, input the pass-code.
   - Other: Signs up for a covert network. Type in the password, security type, and name of the hidden network.
   - If the Wi-Fi icon displays at the upper section of the screen, the iPad is linked to Wi-Fi services (launches Safari and view a webpage to verify this.) As soon as you get back to the same place, the iPad reconnects.

Connecting your gadget to a cellular network (Wi-Fi + Cellular models)

If a Wi-Fi network isn't accessible, your iPad instantly joins the cellular data network of your carrier. If your gadget refused to connect, try out the subsequent:

1. Confirm your SIM is activated & opened.
2. Navigate to Settings > Mobile Data.

Check to see if Cellular Data is enabled.

1. Attempt to link up the most current Wi-Fi network that is accessible.
2. Connect to the selected Wi-Fi network from a catalog of accessible networks.
3. (Wi-Fi + Cellular models) Establishes a connection to your carrier's cellular data network.

CHAPTER 4

Managing Apple ID setup on iPad.

Log in using your Apple ID.

Follow the instructions below if you did not log in during setup:

1. Access Settings.
2. Select Sign in to iPad.
3. Type in your password and ID.
4. You will be able to generate an ID if you don't already have one.
5. Input the 6-digit confirmation code if you have two-factor authentication enabled for your account.

Modify the Apple ID setups.

1. Go to [your name] > Settings in step 1.
2. Execute any of the subsequent:
   - Refresh your contact details
   - Make a new password.
   - Change the Account Recovery Contacts list
   - Managing and viewing your membership Update your billing information or payment methods
   - Family Sharing management.

CHAPTER 5

iCloud

How to use iCloud on iPad

Make iCloud settings changes.

1. Select iCloud under Settings > [your name].
2. Execute any of the subsequent:
3. View the status of your iCloud storage.
4. Activate the functions you wish to use, including Contacts, Photos, Mail, and Messages.

Subscribe to iCloud+ on the iPad

What's included with iCloud+

On an iPad, you can perform the following when you sign up for iCloud+:

1. Purchase 50, 200, or 2 TB of storage.
2. Use Hide My Email to create one-of-a-kind, random email addresses that go to your inbox. See How to Hide My Email in iPad Mail and How to Hide My Email on iPad Safari.
3. Use Private Relay to browse the web even more privately and securely (beta).
4. Install home security cameras with HomeKit Secure Video to enable remote viewing of your footage while maintaining its privacy and security.

5. Use a custom email domain to personalize iCloud Mail. See Set up a custom email domain with iCloud Mail on iPad.

Upgrade, modify or cancel your iCloud+ membership.

1. Select iCloud under Settings > [your name]
2. Select an option and adhere to the on-screen directions after tapping Manage Storage and Change Storage Plan.

CHAPTER 6

Apps and Settings on the iPad

Searching for Settings on the iPad

You can look for iPad settings, like your passcode, notification tones, and more, in the Setup application.

1. the Home Screen, then select Settings (or in the Application Library)
2. To access the search area, slide downward via the upper section of the screen, type "notification," for instance, and then click a setup on the left flank of the display screen.

Setting mail, contacts, and schedule accounts on the iPad

Register a mail account.

1. To include an account, navigate to Setup > Mail > Accounts.
2. Choose one of these:
   - Enter your email account credentials after selecting an email service, like iCloud or Microsoft Exchange.

- To create a new account, touch Other, press Add Mail Account, and then fill out the form.

Setting up your contact's account

1. Select Other under Add Account in Settings > Contacts > Accounts.
2. Enter your server and account information after selecting Add LDAP Account or Include a CardDAV account (if your company supports it).

Setting up/Creating your calendar account

1. Navigate to Settings > Calendar > Accounts to include a new account.
2. After selecting Other, choose from the following:
   - Add an account for a calendar: hit on include CalDAV Account & input your server & account details
   - Register to receive iCal (.ics) calendars: When prompted, either move an ICS folder via Mail or input the URL for the ICS file you want to subscribe to after selecting Add Subscribed Calendar.

Deleting applications you not using on iPad

If your iPad is running slowly, the problem is probably with the RAM rather than the storage.

If your gadget memory is already nearing full capacity, deleting apps you infrequently or never utilized can help. Here's how you will able to delete a Deleting applications you not using on iPad

1. Launch the Settings application, hit on General, then click iPad memory/storage all over.
2. Now, hit on an application you intend to erase & click on Remove Application once the preference appears.

Turn off the background application refresh

1. Open the Settings application, choose General, and after that hit on Background Application Refresh.

2. Via here, you will be able to select to turn off the background application restore for every

application, or slide to the bottom of your list of apps and turn them on and off as you see fit.

Move downloaded music to storage

Any iTunes or Apple Music you've downloaded to your iPad is another storage issue you might want to think about dumping to your external hard drive. To see the amount of your gadgets memory your Music app is using:

1. Launch your Settings application
2. Hit on General.
3. Hit on iPad memory/ Storage.
4. Slide downward and tap Music.
5. You'll see the amount of storage used in the Documents and Data section; In my case, it is only 33KB in size.

Clear Browser Cache, Cookies, and Web History

1. Launch the Settings application.
2. Hit on Safari.
3. Hit on erase History & Website Data.

Change iPad graphic setup

These settings can be changed to save processing power and speed up your iPad; To achieve this:

1. Launch the Settings application.
2. Click Accessibility.
3. Click Display & Text Size.
4. Toggle to reduce transparency.
5. Go back to "Accessibility" and click on "Movement".
6. Toggle between Reduce Motion and Prefer Crossfade Transitions.

Turn off Siri and Search

However, the upside is that turning these features off will save the processing power they require to index each item on your iPad. To disable this feature:

1. Launch the Settings application.
2. Click Siri and Search.
3. This is where this takes a lot of time, but again, having the ability to decide which of your apps you want Siri & Search to turn on or off will allow you to leave basic searches running while turning off apps you don't want. needs indexing.

4. If you want to disable Allow notifications, Show
   in-app library and Spotlight, Show when
   sharing, and Show when listening, turn off all
   four.

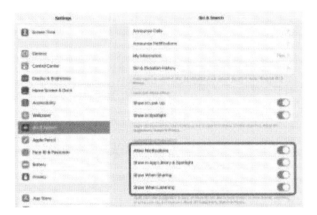

5. Now, tap on any app in Suggestions and turn
   off Show in App, Show on Home Screen, App
   Suggestion, and Notification Suggestion.

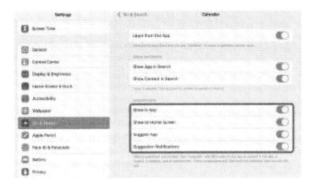

CHAPTER 7

How to turn the iPad floating keyboard on and off

How to operate iPad floating keyboard

1. Launch any keyboard-compatible software, such as the Notes app.

2. Touch & hold down the keyboard symbol at the bottom right angle of your keyboard.
3. A list will appear. Keep your finger on the screen and drag it to select the floating keyboard option.
4. By tapping and dragging the grab bar at the bottom, you may move the floating keyboard across the screen.

How to get rid of the floating keyboard on iPad

1. Grab the bar beneath the floating keyboard and move it to the center of the screen's bottom to return to the standard keyboard.
2. The floating iPad keyboard's center can also be used to make a reverse pinch gesture. Starting close together, your fingers should gradually spread apart while staying in close proximity to the iPad screen the entire time.

CHAPTER 8

Security & unlock iPad

Unlock iPad security using Face ID

1. Tap the display before turning to face your iPad.
2. To show that the iPad is unlocked, the lock icon switches from locked to unlocked
3. To access the home screen, slide upward via the lower section of the display screen.

To lock the iPad again,

1. Click the top button first. If you haven't tapped the iPad's screen for approximately 60 seconds, it locks itself. However, the iPad won't be muted or locked when it sense concentration when attention detection features are enabled in Setups/settings > Face ID & Passwords.

iPad password unlock

1. Click the Home knob (if using an iPad) or slide up from the lock screen's bottom (on others versions).
2. Type in the access key.
3. Click the upper button to lock the iPad once more. The iPad screen locks itself after about a minute of inactivity.

CHAPTER 9

Connect your iPad to the Internet

Connect iPad to Wi-Fi

1. Select Settings > Wi-Fi, then toggle Wi-Fi on.
2. Pick one of the aforementioned buttons.
   - Network: If asked, enter the password.
   - Other: Sign up for a secret network. Type in the password, security type, & designation of the hidden network.
   - Your device will be linked to a Wi-Fi network if the Wi-Fi icon shows at the upper section of the display/screen. (To verify this, launch Safari and see a website.) The iPad reconnects when it gets to similar spots

The Wi-Fi + Cellular models of the iPad require you to connect to a cellular network.

If Wi-Fi is not available, your iPad will automatically connect to your carrier's cellular data network. Attempt the following if the iPad won't connect::

Make sure your SIM card is enabled & opened

1. Select Mobile Data under Settings.

2. Verify that mobile data is toggled on.

Managing mobile data service

1. Select Mobile data under Settings.
2. Execute any of the subsequent
   - Toggle data off & limit all data use to Wi-Fi.
   - Toggle roaming and LTE on/off: Then select Cellular Data Options.
   - Activate your hotspot: Touch Activate your hotspot (offered by some carriers), then adhere to the on-screen directions.
   - Manage your cellular phone account: Carrier Services or Manage [account name] should be selected.

CHAPTER 10

Set up screen

Setting up your screen lock

1. Select the lock screen or home screen image under Settings > Wallpaper, then
2. Hit on Perspective Zoom to enable perspective zoom for the wallpaper you've previously selected.

Manually modify screen brightness

Try one of the following to make your iPad's screen darker or brighter:

1. First, launch Control Center, then press the Brightness button downward.
2. Drag the slider after going to Settings > Display & Brightness

Automatically edit screen brightness

Using a integral ambient light sensor, the iPad adjusts screen brightness based on ambient illumination.

1. Select Accessibility under Settings.

2. Select Text size and display options, then enable Auto-brightness.

Schedule automated activation and deactivation of dark mode

In the settings, you can program the dark mode to start up routinely at nighttime (or on a precise schedule).

1. Select Display & Brightness under Settings.
2. Select Options after activating Auto.
3. You can select a custom schedule or dusk to dawn.
4. When you select Custom Schedule, press the options to choose the periods for activating and deactivating dark mode.

Program night shift to switch on/off automatically

To ease eye strain when watching a screen at night, Night Shift moves the colors to the warmer region of the spectrum.

1. Select Night Shift under Settings > Display & Brightness.
2. programmed activation.
3. Move the slider under Color temperature to the warmer or colder end of the spectrum to alter the color balance for Night Shift.
4. Tap From and choose From dusk to dawn or a custom period.

5. If you select Custom Schedule, tap Options to enter the start and stop hours for Night Shift.
6. Your iPad will use clock and geolocation information to establish the time that works for you if you choose Dusk to Dawn

Switching True Tone on/off

On supported devices, True Tone automatically modifies the hue and brightness of the screen to fit the surrounding lighting.

Attempt one of the following:

1. To toggle on/off True Tone, launch Control Center, press & grip down Brightness button, and then click the True Tone knob.
2. Select Display & Brightness from the Settings menu, then toggle True Tone on or off.

Activate low-power mode

Use of Low Power Mode can result in a longer battery life. Go into low power mode if your iPad's battery is low or you don't have access to a power source.

1. Select Battery under Settings.
2. Enable the low power setting.

Zoom in on your iPad's display for a larger view

Using Screen Zoom, you will be able to make the screen display larger.

1. Select Display & Brightness under Settings.
2. Select View (under screen magnification).
3. Click Set after selecting Zoomed.

Renaming your iPad.

Using iCloud, AirDrop, Personal Hotspot, & your PC, you will be able to rename your iPad.

1. Select Name under Settings > General > About.
2. After typing a new name and selecting Done, hit the Clear Text button.

Modifying/editing your date & time on your gadget

1. Select Date and Time under Settings > General.
2. Turn on any of the subsequent:
   - Automatically set: The iPad adjusts the time based on your current time zone and obtains the accurate time through the network. The iPad might not be able to routinely sense the local time in some nations or areas because some networks do not support network time.
   - 24-Hour Format: (Not accessible in all nations or counties) iPad shows the time via zero to twenty-three.

Modifying language & states on your gadget

1. Select Language and Region under General in Settings.
2. Set the subsequent:
   - Language for iPad,
   - Region,
   - Calendar, and
   - Temperature Unit (Celsius or Fahrenheit)
3. To add a keyboard for a different language, choose Add new keyboard under Settings > General > Keyboard > Keyboards.

CHAPTER 11

Widgets

Adding Widgets on iPad

Your home screen should have a widget.

1. Start by going to the home display screen where the widget will be added. Then, tap and hold the wallpaper there pending when the applications begin to vibrate.
2. To access the widget gallery, hit on the Add Widget knob via the upper section of the screen.
3. After finding the tool you want by scrolling or searching, tap it and then slide leftward & rightward to see the available sizes.
4. Information is displayed in various sizes. Hit on the Add Widget once you find the desired size.
5. Move the widget to the desired location on the screen while the apps are still shaky, and then hit Done.

Editing Widget

1. To enter the Quick Actions list of options, touch and hold a widget on your home screen.
2. If Edit Tool or Edit Stack appears, select Options. If Smart Stack is present, click Edit Tool.
3. You can toggle Smart Rotate or Widget on or off for Smart Stack, drag a widget from the stack to the home display screen, or remove a widget by clicking - in the top-left corner.
4. When you enable suggested widgets, depending on your prior activity suggested widgets for apps you're already using will automatically show in your Smart Stack at the appropriate moment. You have the choice of adding a widget to your collection so that it is always available when you need it.
5. Press "Done."

Take a widget off your home screen

1. To access the quick action menu, press & hold down the tool.
2. Click Remove, then press Remove Widget (or Remove Stack).

Displaying iPad widget when locked

1. Click one of the following choices under Settings, depending on your model:
   - Passcode and Face ID
   - Passcode and Touch ID
   - Access key
   - Type in your access password.
2. Launch Today's View and Search (beneath permit access whenever it is locked).

CHAPTER 12

Utilizing Apple Pencil with iPad

Setting up Pencil

1. Open the back cover of your Pencil if it is a first-generation model and connect the Pencil to the iPad.

2. When you own a 2nd-generation Pencil, use the magnetic connector to fasten it to the iPad's side (All you need to do is fasten the Apple Pencil to the iPad's side). Go to step 5 if it connects automatically.

3. Click pair.

4. You will now be able to configure your Pencil.
5. Hit on Settings.

6. Scroll down and tap on Pencil.

7. Here you can see how much your Apple Pencil charges and adjust its settings.

8. Turn on drawing with the Apple Pencil only if you prefer to navigate your device with your fingers and use the Apple Pencil only to draw or write.

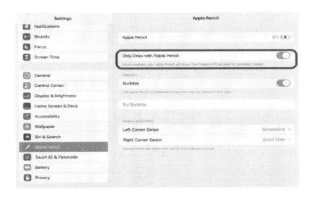

9. Turn on Scribble to convert any handwritten text into a text area for writing.

10. Touch Scribble Experience to practice typing in a text field and converting it to text.

11. Tap the swipe in the left corner to turn your Apple Pencil screenshot on or off. Once toggled on, this gesticulation will work if you only have a drawing with the Apple Pencil turned on.

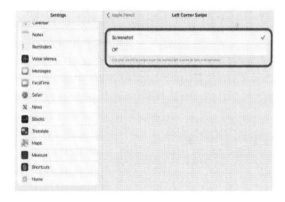

12. Hit on the swipe in the right angle to turn opening Quick Note with Apple Pencil on or off. When turned on, this gesture will work even if you only have a drawing with the Apple Pencil turned on.

When your Pencil refuses functioning properly

1. Charge up your Pencil
2. Restart the app
3. Make sure your Pencil is supported
4. Secure the tip of the Apple Pencil
5. Restart your iPad
6. Make sure Bluetooth is turned on
7. Repair your Apple Pencil
8. Make a call across to Support

Apple Pencil tips and tricks

Here are some cool features that you might not know about Apple Pencil:

- Writing on the Apple Pencil has been mastered. When you type with this tool, the tip detects the pressure you are applying as well as your speed. The iPad then adjusts the stroke weight of the pen, just as if you were using a real pen.

- The iPad detects when you're utilizing your hand & once you're utilizing the Pencil, ensuring daily tasks is easy.
- The iPad will be able to sense your handwriting as words, allowing you to search for phrases you've written with your Apple Pencil.
- The Apple Pencil has a large battery, and if it runs out for a short period it will give you several minutes of use.
- When using the Apple Pencil, which was designed to mimic the experience of using a traditional pencil, accomplishes that goal par excellence. You will be able to switch via utilizing your finger and your Apple Pencil as often as you like without disconnecting it or changing the settings. iPad automatically recognizes the change and adjusts its responses accordingly

CHAPTER 13

How to connect an iPad to an Apple Pencil

Pair/Connect your iPad and second-generation Apple Pencil.

1. Position the Pencil close to the flank of your gadget containing the volume buttons. It will routinely affix to your gadget.

2. A connection prompt will appear at the upper section of the iPad's display/screen.
3. Click on the prompt.
4. Now the 2nd-generation Apple Pencil is paired with the iPad

Pairing 1ˢᵗ gen Pencil to your gadget

1. Remove the cover via your Pencil & connect it to the Lightning port on your gadget.

2. The pairing button will appear.
3. Press the pair button.

Checking your Pencil battery levels

Once you link your Pencil, every time you plug it in, a message will appear showing the battery level of your Apple Pencil. Alternatively, you can slide downward via the upper section of your iPad to see Control Center, where it will display the battery levels of your various connected devices.

Charge your 2ⁿᵈ generation pencil

1. Put the stylus on the flank of the gadget that has the volume buttons. It should turn on and a prompt at the top of the iPad screen will show you that your Apple Pencil is now charging.

Charge your Apple Pencil (1st generation)

1. With a first-generation Apple Pencil, you can connect it using the Lightning port on your

iPad, or use the charging adapter that came with your Apple Pencil.

Open the Notes app with the Apple Pencil

You can simply touch the iPad screen with your Apple Pencil and then start drawing or taking notes. This can even be done from the lock screen.

How to use and customize Double Tap for Apple Pencil

Simply use your finger to double-tap near the tip of your Apple Pencil to switch to the previous tool, then double-tap again to return when you're ready.

You can customize the double-tap feature, which allows you to open the color palette and switch between the current or last used tool on Apple Pencil. To do this:

1. Launch the Settings application on your iPad.
2. Click on the Apple Pencil.
3. Select the double-click option you prefer.

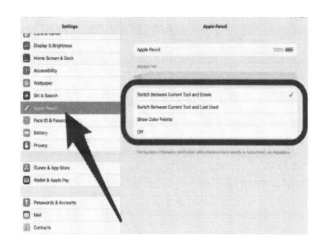

CHAPTER 14

Stage manager on iPad Pro

Turning on ipad's stage manager

Stage Manager is not by default activated with iPadOS 16. Instead, you must activate it via the Control Center or the Settings app.

Utilizing Settings app

1. On your iPad, select the Settings application.
2. Select Multitasking & Home Screen.
3. At the bottom of the Home Panel & Multitasking screen, tap Stage Manager.
4. Turn on the iPad's stage manager.

Stage Manager organizes your launched applications into a strip on the left flank of the screen in iPadOS 16 for easy access. Your apps look larger on the tablet's display while Recent Apps or the Dock are hidden. These options are easy on/off-able.

Control Center usage

On a compatible device, you can also activate Stage Manager using Control Center.

1. To open the Control Center, pull your finger downward via the upper right angle of the display screen.
2. To activate, click the Stage Manager icon.

3. The Stage Manager icon in Control Panel allows you to toggle the Dock and Recent Apps on and off.

Via the left flank of the gadget's screen, after you launch Stage Manager, you'll see icons for your four most recent apps.

Turning off the Stage Manager

Stage Manager may always be turned off in the Control Center or Settings application. However, using Control Center is the simplest method to accomplish this. To do this:

1. To launch the Control Center, pull your finger down from the upper-right angle of the display screen.
2. Squeeze the Stage Manager symbol firmly.
3. Select Turn Stage Manager off.

Resizing apps with the stage manager

The ability to resize the apps on the screen is one of Stage Manager's primary capabilities. You can use this to organize a sometimes jumbled iPad screen.

Resizing applications

1. On the app that is open and active, press and holds the indicator that is visible in the bottom right corner.
2. To change a window's size, use your fingers or the mouse.

Application groups with stage manager

Most likely, you intend to use more than one iPad app at once. Stage Manager's ability to organize apps makes this possible. To do this:

1. Start by opening the first app you want to group.
2. Next, drag & drop the second app into the main screen from the Recent Apps section OR the Dock.

Ungrouping apps with stage manager

You can ungroup apps on your iPad in a matter of seconds if you no longer want to do so:

1. To ungroup an app, start by tapping it.
2. Select the three horizontal dots in the app's top center.
3. Click Minimize to delete the program from the collection.

CHAPTER 15

Camera/videos and selfie taking on your device

How to easily access the ipad camera

Since there is a button for it there, opening the Camera app directly from the Lock Screen is the simplest option. To switch directly to a selfie, video, Portrait mode, or Portrait selfie, you can also use the Control Center Camera toggle or even Haptic Touch.

Methods for utilizing the camera quickly from the Lock screen

1. Tap any location on the Lock-screen.
2. Select the Camera option by tapping the knob in the down right angle of the screen display.
3. You may also open the Camera by just swiping left.

Using camera via Control Center

1. You will be able to instantly click into the Camera application from Control Center and use all of its capabilities.
2. Slide downward via the upper-right angle of the screen on your ipad with Face ID.
3. To access the Camera app, tap the Camera icon in step 3.

4. Snap your photo
5. On supported smartphones that support 3D Touch, you will be able to also access a menu to quickly access the front-facing camera, video recording, slow-motion recording, and portrait mode. On smartphones without 3D Touch, you can access the front-facing camera and record a video. To access further choices, press the Camera button firmly.

You may even ask Siri to assist you in taking a photo if you like using voice commands.

How to use Siri to capture a picture

You can ask Siri to launch one of the three available photo selections in the Camera app.

1. To call Siri or activate her, click & holddown the Home knob/button on your iPad.
2. Speak the phrases "Take a picture," "Take a square picture," or "Take a panorama." The Camera app will launch with the requested setting.
3. Snap a photo.

How to Record a Video

One of the three available video options will be opened in the Camera app when you ask Siri to do so.

1. To call Siri or activate her, click & holddown the Home knob/button on your iPad.
2. Invoke the taking of a video, a slow-motion movie, or a time-lapse video. The Camera app will launch with the requested setting.
3. Take a video.

Taking a selfie

1. To call Siri or activate her, click & holddown the Home knob/button on your iPad.
2. Suggest taking a selfie. The front FaceTime camera in the Camera app will start up.
3. Take a picture or a video of your lovely face grinning.

CHAPTER 16

How to take photos, panoramas, bursts, and more

How to shoot pictures

1. Via the Home screen of your iPad, launch the Camera application.
2. Press the shutter button twice.
3. To examine and adjust your photo, use the Thumbnail button.

How to shoot pictures with the volume button

1. Via the Home display-screen, open the Camera app.
2. As is customary, frame the scene you want to capture.
3. To open the shutter and capture a photo, click the hardware volume-up knob/button.

How to capture pictures with the headphones' remote

1. Via the Home display-screen, open the Camera application.
2. As is customary, frame the scene you want to capture.
3. To start the camera shutter and snap a photo, press the hardware volume up button on the headset.

Taking & capturing images in "burst mode"

1. Start your iPad's Camera app.
2. Use a standard frame to capture the scene you desire.
3. To capture in Burst mode, quickly press and swipe to the left.
4. iOS will choose the image that it deems to be the finest of the lot. You can make your selection if you don't like what you selected.
5. Following burst capture, tap the thumbnail in the down left angle.
6. Tap the stack of burst mode images you wish to view.
7. Hit on Choose
8. Select the photos you want to keep by tapping the blue checkmark.
9. For the photos with the best focus and composition, a gray dot appears below the thumbnail scrubber.

10. When you've decided what to keep, tap Done.
11. Select Keep Everything or Keep Only (number) Favorites to keep only the photographs you've chosen, respectively, and delete the rest of the images in the stack.
12. The chosen pictures are now ungrouped and in your Camera Roll.

How to adjust the iPad's flash

1. Start your iPad's Camera app.
2. Click the Flash switch in the top corner.
3. Decide if you want it to be on Auto, On, or Off. To access the Auto, On, or Off options on an iPad you might need to tap the arrow at the top.

How to configure the iPad camera's timer

1. Open the Camera application on your iPad
2. Click the arrow at the upper section of the screen
3. Press the Timer button.
4. Either 3 or 10 seconds are acceptable
5. Start the countdown by tapping the camera shutter button.

How to change the iPad's rear-facing camera to the front-facing one

1. Start your iPad's Camera app.

2. To switch between the front-facing FaceTime camera and the rear-facing camera, tap the Flip camera button.
3. Press the Shutter button to begin shooting a picture or a video.

Taking square photos on your iPad

1. Start your iPad's Camera app.
2. Swipe up from the area above the shutter button or click the arrow at the upper of the screen.
3. Click the knob/button for the aspect ratio.
4. Choose Square.

Utilizing your iPad to snap a panorama

1. Start your iPad's Camera app.
2. To switch to Pano mode, swipe left twice.
3. If necessary, press the arrow button to alter the direction of the capture.
4. Press the shutter button to begin capturing a panorama.
5. Rotate or pan your iPad to take as many pictures as you'd like of your surroundings. Attempt to maintain alignment between the arrow's point and the yellow guidance. If you're moving too quickly or slowly, the app will let you know.

To end the panorama, press the shutter button one more time.

CHAPTER 17

Live picture

How to apply live photo filters with the iPad camera

1. Start your iPad's Photos app.
2. Slide up from above the shutter button or click the arrow at the upper section of the screen.
3. Press the filter button, which resembles three offset circles.
4. Decide which filter to apply.
5. Press the shutter button to take a picture while the filter is in place.

How to use your ipad to take a live photo

1. Via the Home display-screen, open the Camera application.
2. To turn on Live Photo, tap the top-center button (which resembles a pair of diffusing rings) (yellow).
3. To take your Live Photo, tap the shutter button.
4. A yellow LIVE label will appear and the Live Photo icon will animate with a brief ripple to indicate that it is on.

A yellow LIVE label will appear and the Live Photo symbol will animate with a brief ripple to indicate that it is on.

1. Launch the Photos application on your iPad.
2. Look for the Live Photo that you intend to see.
3. Press & hold down the picture to animate it.

How to use your ipad to share live photos

1. Via the Home display-screen, open the Photos app.
2. Navigate to the Live Photo you want to share and hit it. You can tell if a photo is Live by the gray "Live" symbol in the upper left angle of your display screen.
3. On your screen, click the Share option in the lower left corner. It appears to be a box with an upward-pointing arrow.
4. Select a sharing approach. You may upload your GIFS to YouTube as well as practically every other social networking site.
5. Use the method of your choosing and follow the on-screen instructions to share it just like you normally would.

Setting a live photo as the wallpaper

you can set Live Photos as your wallpaper, which works particularly well for loved ones, kids, pets, and landscapes.

1. Via the Home display-screen, launch the Photos application.
2. Locate the Live Photo that you want to set as your background.
3. Press the Share icon.
4. Select "Use as Wallpaper" from the menu.
5. If it isn't already selected, tap Live Photo in the lower rightward angle of your screen.
6. Press Set. The size of a Live Photo wallpaper cannot be changed.
7. Choose Set Both, Set Lock Screen, or Set Home Screen from the menu.

How to get a still shot from a live photo

You can make a copy of the image if you only want the image and not the fancy moving component.

1. Launch the Photos app.
2. Choose the Live Photo from which you wish to capture a still image.
3. Hit on the Share knob/button in the lower left-hand angle of the display.
4. In the choice tray at the lower section of the display-screen, select Duplicate.
5. Select Copy as Still Photo.

How to make a gif from a live photo

1. Via the Home display-screen, launch the Photos application.

2. Locate and press the Live Photo you want to convert to a GIF from.
3. To access the animation settings, slide upward via the lower section of the screen
4. If you want the Live Photo to loop as a GIF, tap Loop. Long exposure or even "Bounce" it like the Instagram Boomerang app are more options

How to make a video by stitching together many live photos

1. Start Photos on your iPad
2. Locate the Live Photos that you wish to use to produce a movie file.
3. If an image has the diffusing circle icon and the word "LIVES" next to it in the top left corner when you are viewing it, it is a Live Photo.
4. Press the Share icon.
5. Just above the options for the Share Sheet, you can navigate through your photographs and choose more.
6. Select Save as Video by scrolling down.

The Recents album will contain your brand-new video.

CHAPTER 18

How to geo-locate your photos, bias exposure, enable grid, and lock focus

How to lock the exposure and focus

1. From your Home screen or Lock screen, open the Camera app.
2. Use your finger to click the screen to choose the area of the picture you wish to expose and concentrate on.
3. Press & holddown your focal point until you see an AE/AF Lock banner at the upper section of the screen to lock exposure and focus.
4. Once you're ready to capture your picture, press the shutter knob.
5. You can unlock the focus and exposure at any time by tapping anywhere on the screen.

How to bias exposure

1. From your Home screen or Lock screen, open the Camera app.
2. To activate the focus point, tap anywhere on the live preview.
3. Hold the exposure button that appears next to it by tapping and holding (it looks like the

Sun). A slider that lets you change the exposure will now be visible.

4. To make the image lighter or darker, drag your finger up or down to increase or decrease the exposure bias.

Activating grid lines

You can enable the camera grid in Settings if you need a little assistance in creating the "rule of thirds" for your photographs.

1. Launch the Settings application on your iPad's Home screen.
2. Click Camera & Photos. To find it, you need to scroll down a bit.
3. To activate the Grid, tap the switch next to it. It's under the Camera section, almost halfway down.

How to Turn on GPS Geolocation

1. Launch the Settings application on iPad via the Home screen.
2. Click on Privacy
3. Choose Location Services.
4. Select Camera
5. Select Whether to Use the App Now or Never.

CHAPTER 19

Recording video, slow-mo, and time lapses

Utilizing your device to record video

1. Start your iPad's Camera app.
2. To enter video mode, tap on the Video button or swipe right.
3. Press the red "Record" knob/button to begin recording.
4. To stop the video, tap the red Stop button.

Everything you photograph is automatically stored in the photo library on your device.

How to alter the frame rate and resolution of a video

1. Open the Settings app.
2. Click Camera when you scroll down.
3. Choose Record Video.
4. Select the resolution and frame rate you want.

Additional features like Auto Low Light FPS and Lock Camera might also be available on more recent models. In order to improve low-light footage and avoid moving between cameras when recording, this automatically lowers the frame rate from 30 to 24 fps.

How to record slo-mo video on an iPad

1. Start your iPad's Camera app
2. Either swipe right twice (if the Photos mode is selected by default) or press the Slo-Mo button in the bottom left.
3. Press the Record button to start filming in slow motion.
4. Hit on the Stop button to stop/end the recording.

How to adjust the slo-mo video's slow and regular speed points

1. Start Photos on your iPad.
2. Find the slow-motion video you wish to edit.
3. If you want to find Slo-mo quickly, you may always scroll down in the Albums part of the website.
4. To watch the slow-motion video, tap on it.
5. Click Edit. The slo-mo segment of the chronology is expanded as a result.
6. To indicate when the video should gradually transition into and out of slow motion, simply touch and move the sliders at both ends.
7. Tap Done to save your changes when you're finished when you're happy with them.

Simply follow steps 1-4 above if you later decide to revert it to the default setting. But to return to the original after modifying, just tap on Revert.

How to tweak between slo-mo

1. Launch the Settings application on your gadget.
2. Locate the Camera by scrolling down and tapping it.
3. Click on Record Slo-mo.
4. Tap the selection you desire.

How to make a time-lapse video on an iPad

1. Start your iPad's Camera app.
2. After the initial swipe, tap the word "Time Lapse" when it appears. Alternatively, swipe right three times.
3. To start recording your footage, tap the Record button.
4. The longer you film for time-lapse videos, the better the final product will be. Therefore, unwind while the iPad does its thing
5. Press the Stop button to halt recording.

How to use your iPad to shoot a still shot while recording a video

1. Start your iPad's Camera app.
2. Change to video mode and begin filming.
3. To take a photo, press the all-white shutter button to the left of the stop button.

Editing videos

1. On your iPad running, open the Photos app.

2. Locate the video you wish to edit, then press on it to watch.
3. Hit on Edit via the option list in the upper right angle.
4. Simply choose the tool you wish to use in the editing mode and make your modifications as you would with a photo.

When you're finished and pleased with the adjustments, tap Done to save.

CHAPTER 20

Using the telephoto lens on your iPad

Utilize photographic zoom

1. Launch the Camera app, then select Photo, Square, or Pano.
2. Tap the 1x button, then swipe left to zoom in or out and right to zoom out. In Photo or Square, you can expand up to 10x; in Pano, you can increase up to 2x.
3. Tap the zoom button once more to go back to 1x.

Note: With just one push of the zoom button, you may easily go from 1x to 2x zoom.

How to utilize zoom in a video

1. Launch the Camera app and select Video or Slo-Mo from the menu.
2. Tap the 1x button, then swipe left to zoom in or out and right to zoom out. In Slo-Mo or video, you can increase by up to three times, or by two times in time-lapse.
3. Tap the zoom button once more to go back to 1x.

CHAPTER 21

Portrait mode

How to take a portrait or portrait lighting photo of a person

1. Start the Camera app.
2. Slide to the Portrait position.
3. Position your subject between 2 and 8 feet away from the shot you want to take. The face and body identification feature on the camera should instantly recognize your person.
4. Pay attention to the directions in the Camera application (either "More light required," "Flash may help," "Place subject within 8 feet," or "Move farther away.")
5. The banner at the upper section will change to yellow if you've satisfied the camera's requirements.

Note: Even if the placard refuses to turn yellow, you may still use the telephoto lens in Portrait mode; however, you won't get any depth or lighting effects.

6. Sliding or pressing the cube icons above the shutter button will allow you to change your lighting effects in real-time.
7. To snap a picture, press the shutter button.

How to change the intensity of portrait lighting

1. Slide to the pictures application on your gadget
2. View a photo taken in Portrait Mode.
3. Click Edit.
4. If you didn't choose portrait lighting when you took the original photo, choose one now.
5. To lessen or intensify the lighting effect, slide leftward or rightward on the adjustment bar. The bar automatically begins at 50.
6. Click Done.

How to delete the depth effect from images taken in portrait mode

1. Click on the Photo application.
2. Click the Portrait Mode picture that you want the Depth Effect removed from.
3. Pick Edit via the option list in the upper right.
4. Via the upper section of the display screen, hit on Portrait. The Depth Effect will no longer exist as a result. To bring it back, tap it once more.

CHAPTER 22

Take manual mode and raw photos

TURN ON PRORAW

1. Open Settings.
2. Click Camera after swiping down.
3. Click Formats.
4. Ensure that Apple ProRAW is turned on (green).

CHAPTER 23

How to rapidly edit and share pictures and movies taken using the iPad's Camera app

How to share and edit pictures and videos fast

1. From your Home screen or Lock screen, open the Camera app, and take a picture.
2. Hit on the thumbnail button/knob in the lower leftward angle.
3. Decide on an action.
4. Tap the Share icon to open the AirDrop, chat, and social media menus.
5. Press the heart-shaped Favorite button to add a photo to your Favorites album.
6. Tap the Edit button to access features like Markup, filters, cropping and clipping, and red-eye reduction.
7. To remove the image or video, first, tap the Trash icon.
8. Use the Scrubber bar to choose a different photo by tapping it.

Using Night mode

1. Launch the Camera app.
2. Get ready to snap the photo you wish to take.
3. Press the Shutter key.
4. While the picture is being shot, keep still. A timer will appear so you will be able to view the time frame a shot takes
5. To view how it turned out, click the thumbnail picture in the bottom-left angle.

How to modify the intensity of the Night mode manually

1. Launch the Camera app.
2. Get ready to snap the photo you wish to take.
3. When the Night mode button displays, tap it.
4. Toggle between turning off Night Mode, maintaining the timer at its default setting, or setting it to the maximum time by swiping the timer dial to the right or left (often 9 or 10 seconds).
5. Click the shutter knob to begin taking photos. While the timer is counting down, keep your hand still.
6. To view how it turned out, click the thumbnail picture in the bottom-left angle.

How to disable Night Mode

1. Launch the Camera app.
2. Click the Night mode button next to the flash icon in the upper-left angle. Once it's off, the icon will turn gray.
3. Snap your photo

CHAPTER 24

USING DND

Utilizing DND in Control Center

DND can be enabled or disabled whenever you want from the Control Center. Your regularly planned Do Not Disturb time won't be impacted by this.

1. On your iPad via Face ID, slide downward from the upper right angle of the display screen. On previous iPad version, slide upward via the lower section of the screen.
2. To activate Do Not Disturb, tap the Moon icon. The logo will be purple and the icon will turn white.
3. Tap the Moon symbol to switch off Do Not Disturb. Transparency will appear in the icon.

Setup Do not disturb mode when driving

You may fight the urge to use your phone while driving by setting your phone to "Do Not Disturb" mode. This turns off all notifications, including incoming calls and text messages, right from Control Center.

1. Slide downward via the top-right angle of the display screen on an tablet with Face ID. Slide upward via the lower section of the screen on other model
2. To be able to activate "Do Not Disturb" when driving, tap the automobile symbol. The logo will be purple and the icon will turn white. The color of the Do Not Disturb logo will also change.
3. To be able to deactivate "Do Not Disturb" When driving, tap the automobile symbol. Transparency will appear in the icon.

Control Center Flashlight

The Flashlight is easily accessible in Control Center. Only iPads with flashlights can access it.

1. On your iPad via Face ID, slide downward via the topo- right angle of the screen. On previous iPad version, slide upward via the lower section of the screen.
2. To activate the flashlight, click the Flashlight symbol. A blue logo will appear on the white symbol. A back LED light will also come on.
3. To turn off the flashlight, tap the Flashlight icon. The LED light will go out, and the icon will become transparent.

CHAPTER 25

Haptic touch

How to use haptic touch to view actions on the home screen

1. Press the Home screen icon for which you wish to open quick actions for a long time (Haptic Touch).
2. Hit on the command you intend carrying out.
3. Dynamic actions function in the same way, with the exception that the task's subject will alter depending on the time, place, and other variables.
4. Press the Home screen icon for which you wish to open quick actions for a long time (Haptic Touch).
5. Hit on the command you intend carrying out.
6. There are unique quick actions designed just for downloading apps, such as giving one app priority over all others, halting downloads, and canceling them.
7. Press the installation symbol of the software you wish to open rapid actions for a long (Haptic Touch).
8. Hit on the command you intend carrying out.

9. Haptic Touch actions are also available for folders. By default, you have the option to rename the folder; however, if an app has a notification badge, you can view the count and press directly to launch it without opening the folder.
10. Press the Home screen folder for which you wish to show quick actions for a long time (Haptic Touch).
11. Press the action button to complete it.

How to Haptic Touch to Animate a Live Photo

1. Press the Live Photo for a long time to hear and notice it come to life.
2. When viewing all of the images in an album, you can long-press on a Live shot to peek and pop it. Additionally, you have the following options:
   - Copy
   - Share
   - Favorite/unfavorite
   - Display in Every Photo (if you are viewing from a specific album)
   - Delete

CHAPTER 26

Home screen setting

Hide and show home screen pages

1. Click the home display screen & hold down until the apps begin to vibrate.
2. Press the lower section of the display screen's dots.
3. Checkmarks show beneath the thumbnails of the home screen pages.
4. Touch to remove checkmarks to hide pages.
5. Touch to add checkmarks to reveal hidden pages.
6. On your iPad via Face ID, hit Done twice or the Home screen wallpaper twice (on other iPad models).

Rearrange home screen pages

1. Press & holddown the background on your home display screen to make the apps vibrate.
2. Press the bottom of the screen's dots.
3. Checkmarks show beneath the thumbnails of the home screen pages.
4. Click & holddown each page on the Home display screen, then move it to a different location to reposition it.
5. Double-tap Done.

CHAPTER 27

Switching between applications on your gadget

Utilize the app switcher

One of the following actions will display all running programs, split-width workspaces, and sliding windows in the application switcher:

1. Slide upward via the lower section of the display screen on your iPad, then halt in the middle of your display screen.
2. Double-click the Home button on an iPad that has one.
3. Swipe right to browse the list of open apps, then tap the one you intend to utilize or the Split View workspace.
4. You can see Slide Over windows via sliding your finger to the left and switching between them by touching them.

Switching between open applications

Pick any of the subsequent actions to be able to switch via an open applications

1. Slide your finger along the lower border of the display, left or right.

2. Use 4 or 5 fingers to slide leftward or rightward.

Quitting & reopening an application on your iPad

You can try to resolve a problem by closing and reopening an app if it is not responding. (Typically, there is no justification for closing the app; closing it does not, for instance, conserve battery life.)

➢ Open the App Switcher, then slide upward on the application to close it.
➢ Move to the home display screen (or App Library), then press the application to reopen it.

CHAPTER 28

Your Keyboard/trackpad and typing

Type with your iPad's on-screen keyboard.

1. To return to the full-size keyboard, spread your two fingers apart. On the full-size keyboard, you can tap the keys to type.
2. While typing on the full-size keyboard or the mini keyboard, you can do any of the following:
3. Click the Shift knob/button while continuing to scroll to an uppercase letter to type uppercase letters.
4. To activate the caps lock, press Shift twice
5. To swiftly insert a period and a space after the word, hit on the space bar twice (double click)
6. Correct spelling: To see recommended corrections, tap the incorrect word (underlined in red), then tap Suggest. You can also input the correction if you want.
7. Add numbers, punctuation, or symbols as follows: Hit the symbol or number key.
8. To undo the most recent edit, swipe left with three fingers and hit Undo at the upper section of the screen. Alternatively, you may also click the Undo button.

9. To reset last, slide rightward via 3 fingers and select Reset from the menu at the top section of the display-screen. Alternatively, press the Undo button
10. Press the Hide keyboard key to hide the virtual keyboard.

Enter emojis using the on-screen keyboard

- By clicking inside a text box, you can launch the on-screen keyboard.
- Press the Next keyboard, Emoji, or Next keyboard key to toggle to the emoji keyboard.
- Use a popular term, such as "heart" or "smiley face," in the find field at the upper section of the keyboard after tapping the Search symbol in the lower left angle to find an emoji.
- Tap on an emoji to input it
- Swipe over the emoji that appears to view additional alternatives.
- Press ABC in the bottom left angle to return to the standard keyboard.

Turn your on-screen keyboard into a trackpad

1. Use one finger to click & holddown the space bar until the keyboard turns light gray.
2. Drag the insertion point across the keyboard to reposition it.

Released after the keyboard was changed to a trackpad. To indicate that it has been converted to a touchpad, the keyboard has been grayed out.

3. Press the keyboard with a second finger and hold it there to select text. Next, make a selection adjustment by circling the keyboard with your first finger.

Use the split keyboard

Utilize the split keyboard at the lower level of the screen to type, or the un-mounted keyboard in the center of the screen.

1. To activate or deactivate the split keyboard, click & holddown the Emoji keyboard below the key. The split keyboard can be chosen by switching the keyboard key, touching the Keyboard settings, or going to Settings > General > Keyboard and turning the Split keyboard on or off.
2. After turning on the split keyboard in Settings, press and hold the Hide keyboard key while performing one of the following actions:
3. To utilize a split keyboard, move your finger to the Split position, then let go. Alternatively, use

two fingers to spread the keyboard out via the center.

4. Center the screen with the keyboard there: Release your finger after sliding it to Undock.

5. Return to a keyboard with all the keys available: move your finger to the Dock & Merge, then let go.

6. Return to the complete keyboard to the screen's lower area: Backswipe to the Dock, then let go.

Enter accented characters or other characters as you type

1. As you type, click & holddown the letter, number, or symbol associated with the letter you want on the keyboard.

2. You could take any of the following actions:

   - On a Thai keyboard, tap and hold the matching Arabic number to select the original numerals.

   - On a keyboard in Chinese, Japanese, or Arabic: Slide leftward to view additional options, or touch a suggested character or filter above the keyboard to type it.

Activate dictation

1. Navigate to Setups/settings > General > Keyboard.
2. Select activate Dictation.

Dictate the text

1, Press the Dictation key on the on-screen keyboard, then speak.

3. If you don't see the Dictation switch, ensure the switch for Enable Dictation under setups/Settings > General > Keyboard is turned on.
4. When done, touch the keyboard key.
5. The on-screen keyboard displays the Dictation key (to the left of the space bar), which you can tap to start dictating text.
6. To insert text by dictation, click to position the insertion point anywhere you intend to input text, press the Dictation key, and speak. You can also replace the selected text with dictation.

Select, cut, copy and paste text on your device

Select and edit text

Do one of the following actions to select the text

1. Choose a word: Tap with one finger twice.
2. Pick a sentence and triple-tap it with one finger.

3. Pick a paragraph of text: Drag from the first word in the block by double-tapping and holding it.
4. You can write the selection or tap it to see the editing choices after choosing the text you wish to review:
   - Cut: With three fingers, tap Cut or Join twice.
   - Copy: Use three fingers to close by tapping Copy or Disc.
   - Paste: Use three fingers to squeeze or tap open.
   - Replace: Check out the suggested alt text, or request an alternate text from Siri.

Enter text by typing

1. Choose one of the following methods to place an insertion point where you prefer the text to appear:
   - Tap the area where text should be added.
   - To zoom in and reposition the insertion point, click & hold the text, then drag.

A long document can be navigated through by touching and holding the right border of the page, then dragging the track wheel to position the text you wish to read.

2. Input the text that you want to include.
3. A copied/cut Text via another part of the page can likewise be inserted.

Use the predictive text on the iPad

Accept or decline the predictive text suggestion

- As you type, touch the suggested word or emoji to accept it; input a space or a punctuation mark to accept the featured idea.
- A space is added after the word once you press a suggested word. The space is removed when a comma, period, or other punctuation mark is used.
- Click on your original word to reject ideas (displayed as a predictive text preference in quotation marks).

Deactivate predictive text

Via an on-screen keyboard:
1. Turn off prediction by touching and holding the Next keyboard key, Emoji key, or Change keyboard key, then tapping Keyboard options.

Via external keyboard:
1. Disable prediction by going to your gadget setup/Settings > General > Keyboard.

Save keystrokes with text replacement on iPad

Create a text alternative

Try out any of the subsequent:

1. When using an on-screen keyboard, press and hold the Emoji, Change, or Next keyboard key while tapping the Keyboard options, and then hit Replace text.
2. Using an external keyboard: navigate to setups/Settings > General > Keyboard, then hit on the Replace Text icon.
3. Press the Add knob or button at the top rightward angle.
4. Enter the text abbreviation you want to use in the Abbreviation box and a phrase in the Phrase field.

Don't want your words or phrases to be corrected

1. Select Text replacement from the Settings > General > Keyboard menu.
2. Input the text or phrase in the Phrase area after clicking the Add knob or button via the upper- right angle; leave the Acronym field empty.

Resetting your private dictionary

1. Select Reset under Settings > General
2. Hit on Reset keyboard dictionary.
3. The keyboard dictionary is reset to its default settings when all customized words and shortcuts have been deleted.

CHAPTER 29

Adding or modifying your iPad keyboard

Adding or removing a keyboard for an added language

1. Select Keyboard under Settings > General.
2. Choose one of the following after tapping Keyboards:
   - Why not add a keyboard? Select a keyboard via the list after adding a new keyboard. Continue to add keyboards.
   - Remove the keyboard: To delete a keyboard, select Edit, select Delete, select Done, and then select the keyboard.
   - Rearrange the keyboards on your list: Drag the Reorder button next to the keyboard to a different position in the list by tapping Edit, and then press Done.

Switch to another keyboard

On-screen keyboard:
1. Touch and hold the next keyboard, emoji, or Change keyboard, then
2. Click the switch to the desired keyboard name

You can also touch the following keyboard key, Emoji key, or keyboard switch key to switch between keyboards. Keep clicking to access other enabled keyboards.

On an external keyboard:
1. Hold the Control key, then
2. Press Space to switch between English, emoji, and other keyboards you'd add for different languages.

With Magic Keyboard for iPad and Smart Keyboard, you can also press the Switch Keyboard key to switch between keyboards.

Set an alternate keyboard layout
You can utilize a different keyboard layout that does not correspond to the keyboard's key layout.

1. Select Keyboards under Settings > General > Keyboard.
2. Select a language from the menu at the upper section of the display-screen.
3. From the selection, choose an alternative format.

CHAPTER 30

Moving & Copying items via Dragging & Dropping on your gadget

Move an item

1. If it's text, pick it first before touching and holding the object till it opens up.
2. Drag it to another place in the application.
3. If you drag a long document to the lower section or upper section, it will scroll automatically.

Copying an item via opened applications

1. Slide over or open two items in Split View, then tap and hold one of the items pending when it pops up (if it's text, choose it first).
2. Move or slide it to the other application.

Wherever you may place the item, an insert icon displays as you drag. A large page will automatically scroll if you drag it down or up.

CHAPTER 31

Split view

Drag a link to a split view or slide show window

1. Click & holdddown the link pending when it pops up, then try any of the subsequent:
2. Replace the Slide Over or Split View window with the link target: Drag the link into the window.
3. Open link target in split view or sliding window: When split view or sliding window is not displayed, move the link to leftward or rightward edge of the screen to open the target in split view, or drag the link to close it-is. to the edge to open it in Slide Over.

Copy an item to an application on the dock or home screen

1. If the item is text, select it before touching and holding it until it appears.
2. While holding the item, use a second finger to slide upward via the lower border of the display screen, pause, then hit the Home button to bring up the Dock (on an iPad with the Home button).

3. To open the other application, drag the item over it (as you drag it, a ghostly image of the item appears under your finger).
4. Using the app, you can drag items to the location where you wish to put them (as you drag an insert icon appears where you will be able to drop the item). To access the note where you wish to put the item, for instance, swipe across the notes list. You can also use a different finger.

Choose multiple items to move

1. Select the first item by touching it, holding it down while dragging it a little.
2. Click other things with a different finger while holding the initial item. The badge shows how many items have been chosen.
   Drag each component into place.
3. Raise your finger prior dragging or moving objects off the screen if you decide against moving them.

Open Two Items in Split View on iPad

1. Launch a second application in Split View
2. When using an application, click the Multitasking Controls button (the 3 dots at the upper section of the app), then press the Split View button, then click the Left Split View knob/button to display the current app in the application. Leftward flank of the display

screen, or the rightward button Split view to place the current application on the right.

3. The app you're using slides to the side to reveal your Home screen and Dock.
4. Search for the second application you intend to launch and tap it from your Home screen or the Dock.
5. Split View displays both applications

Replace App in Split View

You will be able switch out one of the open applications once you have two opened application in Split View.

1. To replace it, scroll down via the multitasking controls button at the upper section of the program (the 3-dots at the upper part of the application).
2. Drop the application you intend to replace, and the other app slides to the side to reveal the Home screen and Dock.
3. Find the alternative application on your home display/screen or in the Dock, then tap on it.
4. The two apps appear side by side in Split View.

Go back to full screen

When you have two apps or windows open in Split View, you can remove one and display the other full screen. Do one of the following:

1. Drag the center divider to leftward or rightward of the screen.

2. Click the Multitasking Controls knobs/button at the upper section of the application you want to make full screen, the hit on the Full-Screen knob/button.

3. Touch and hold the multitasking controls button at the top of the app you want to make full screen. Keeping the top edge on the screen, drag it toward the center of the screen until your name and icon appear, then lift your finger.

CHAPTER 32

SLIDE OVER

Change the Application Window to a Slide Window on iPad

1. Launch an application in Slide Over
2. When utilizing an application, click the Multitasking controls button at the upper segment of the display screen, & then click the Slide knob/button.
3. Your Home display screen & Dock are revealed when the app you're using slides to the side.
4. Locate and launch the application you wish to show up in the rear of the **SlideOver** window.

The first app launches, and a **SlideOver** window with the second app displays in front of it.

App Switching in Slide Over

1. Swipe rightward along the Slide Over window's bottom, or carry out the following actions:
2. Via the Slide Over window's bottom, slide upward via the middle of the display screen, pause, and then free your finger.
3. The Slide Over windows all show up.
4. If the desired app is visible, click it.
5. Swipe leftward and rightward through applications to check if you will be able to find them.

Moving the SlideOver Window

Choose one of these:

1. Drag the Multitasking controls button at the upper section of the SlideOver window to drag the SlideOver window to the opposite flank of the display screen.
2. To temporarily conceal a SlideOver window, slide up completely from the bottom, slide the Multitasking Controls button, or move any flank side of the window to the leftward edge of the display screen.
3. Reposition the SlideOver window on the display: via the leftward flank of the display screen, move the tab that is associated with the SlideOver window.

Launch a file in the middle of the display.

Many iPad applications, like as Mail, Messages, Notes, and Files, allow you to open an item at the middle of the application window.

Pick one of these to try:

1. Press down on a mailbox message
2. Touch & hold down a message discussion.
3. Press down on a note in the catalog of notes.
4. Select Open in a new window.

Without altering your current view, the object appears in the center of the screen, over what you are now observing.

See the launched windows & workspaces of the application

See the open windows of the application

Execute any of the following:

1. To show the Dock, slide upward via the lower flank of the screen.
2. Navigate to the home display.
3. Hold down the desired app's window while touching and holding it, then select Show all windows.

Note: All apps will begin to vibrate if you touch and hold them for an extended period. Try again by tapping the Done button or by pressing the Home button (if your iPad has one).

Multitasking with Picture in Picture on iPad

1. When watching a video, press the Picture-in-Picture Home button or click the Home knob (on your iPad with the Home button).
2. The video window shrinks to an angle of your display screen so you will be able to view the home display screen & launch other applications. While viewing the video window, you can do any of the following:

3. Resize the video window: To enlarge the small video window, tap on it to open it. To shrink it back, tap on it to shutdown.
4. Displaying and disabling controls on the video window, tap it.
5. Drag the video window to a different position on the display screen
6. Drag the video window leftward or rightward border of the screen to make it invisible.
7. Click the Close button to close the video window.
8. Go back to the full-screen video: In the tiny video box, select Picture-in-Picture by clicking the button.

Show a preview of notifications on the lock screen.

1. Click Notifications in the Settings section
2. Select Always after selecting Show Previews. Text via messages, message lines via the mail, and information about invitations from the calendar are all included in notification previews

Take Quick Actions on iPad

1. You can view previews, launch quick action menus, & others on the home display screen, in the Control Center, and apps.
2. Touch & hold down an image in Photos to receive a preview and the available options.
3. In Mail, click & hold down a text to view the list of options and a preview of the message's content.
4. To enter the Quick Actions list of option, press & hold down the application symbol on the home display screen for a brief moment. If the icons begin to flicker, select Done in the top-right angle or hit on the Home knob/button (if your iPad has one), then try again.
5. To see the options, press & hold down an item, such as the camera or the brightness control, in Control Center
6. To reply to a notice on the lock display screen, lightly click & hold-down the notification
7. To transform the keyboard into a trackpad while typing, tap and hold down the space bar using a finger.

CHAPTER 33

Using search on iPad

Search using your iPad

1. Choose the apps you want to include in the search
2. Select Siri and Search under Settings.
3. After selecting an app, go down and toggle display in Search on/off.

Searching your iPad

1. Via the Lock-screen or the Home display screen's center, swipe downward.
2. Hit the find box, then input what you intend searching for.
3. Execute any of the subsequent:
   - See additional results on the screen by hiding the keyboard: Select Search.
   - Touch to open the suggested app.
   - Obtain further details about a search suggestion: To open it, click it and then tap one of the outcomes
   - Launch a fresh search: In the search field, click the Clear Text button.

Turning search recommendations off

1. Turn off Suggestions while searching by going to Settings > Siri & Search.

Disable location services for recommendations

1. Select Location Services under Settings > Privacy.
2. Turn off Location-Based Suggestions by tapping System Services.

Find apps

Many applications provide a search bar or button that you may use to find something inside the program. For instance, you can look up a specific area using the Maps app.

1. In an application, hit on or press the Search button (if there is one).
2. Slide downward via the upper section if you are not seeing a search field or button.
3. Input your search term & click Search.

Adding a dictionary

You may install dictionaries on the iPad so you can do searches with them.

1. Select Dictionary under Settings > General.
2. Choose a dictionary.

CHAPTER 34

Airdrop

Send anything with AirDrop on the iPad

1. Click the Share, Share, AirDrop, More Options, or other buttons that display the sharing options for the app after opening the item.
2. Select AirDrop from the list of sharing choices then selects a nearby AirDrop user's profile photo.

Sending Items to Your iPad via airdrop.

1. Launch Control Center, click & holddown the set of controls in the top left corner, then hit the symbol for AirDrop.
2. To select who you want to receive goods from, touch Contacts Only or every-person. Each request that comes in can be approved or denied.

CHAPTER 35

Take a screenshot or record a screen on an iPad

Taking a screenshot

1. Pick via the below list:
   - Press & hold down the upper section & home buttons simultaneously on an iPad with a home button.
   - Using other models: click & hold down any volume knob and the upper section button (located on the top right edge of the device) at the same time.
2. Tap the Done button after tapping the screenshot in the bottom left corner.
3. Select Delete Screenshot, Store to folders, or Save to Photos.

When you select Store to Pictures, you will be able to view them in the All Photos album if utilizing iCloud Photos or the Screenshots album in the Photos application.

Saving a full-page screenshot as a PDF

A web page, document, or email that is longer than the iPad screen can be fully captured or swiped, and then saved as a PDF.

1. Select via the below list:
   - Click & hold down the upper section & home buttons simultaneously on your iPad using a home button.
2. In the bottom leftward angle, select Screenshot. Then select Full Page.
3. Execute any of the subsequent:
   - Save the screen capture: Touch Done hit on Save PDF to a folder, pick a location, then hit on Save.
   - Share the screenshot: Press the Share button, choose a sharing option (for example, AirDrop, Messages, or Mail), input any other necessary details, and then send the PDF.

Make a screen capture/recording video.

On your gadget, you will be able to record a screen and record sound.

1. Click the Insert button subsequent to display Screen Recording after going to setups/Settings > Control Center.
2. Launch Control Center, select the Screen Recording preference, & then watch the three seconds pass.
3. To halt recording, launch Control Center, hit the ruby status bar via the upper section of the screen or the Record Selected Screen button, and then tap Stop.

4. Select Screen Recording under Photos.

CHAPTER 36

Draw using Markup in Apps on iPad

Showing, moving, & hiding the Markup toolbar

1. To display the Markup toolbar in a supported application, click the Show Handwriting Tools button or the Markup button, and then attempt any of the subsequent:

    - Slide the Markup toolbar to any screen edge to reposition it.
    - (Drag from the toolbar's middle edge closest to the screen's middle) (Move via the middle border of the toolbar closest to the center of the screen.)
    - Minimize the toolbar automatically when you draw or enter text: Press the Ellipses button, then turn on the automatic minimization.

2. To unhide the entire toolbar again, click on the mini version.

    - Hide the toolbar: Click the Show Handwriting Tools button or the Done button.

Draw or write on apps with Markup

As you write or draw, try out any of the subsequent:

1. To adjust the line width, tap the drawing tool you want to use in the toolbar and then select an option.
2. To alter the opacity, hit on the sketching tool you intend to utilize in the toolbar and then slide the slider.
3. Modify the hue by selecting a new hue using the hue picker on the Markup toolbar.
4. To correct an error, click the Undo button.
5. To sketch a parallel streak, select the Ruler tool from the toolbar and then trace a line parallel to the ruler's edge.
6. Press & hold down the ruler using 2 fingers, then spin them to alter the ruler's angle.
7. Drag the ruler with one finger to shift it without affecting its angle.
8. Tap the Ruler tool on the toolbar once again to make the ruler invisible.

Change your text or handwritten graphics

1. Select the material you wish to edit by selecting the lasso tool on the Markup toolbar (between the eraser and the ruler).
   - Double-tap on the word or drawn object you've chosen.
   - Select a sentence: Touch it three times.

- Choose a section or block of text: Drag to the last word after touching and holding the first word. Swipe carefully to define more precisely.
- Markup in the Notes app distinguishes between handwritten text and drawn objects, allowing you to select only handwriting. You can also drag images into your selection if you want to.
- Selecting several drawn things requires using the lasso tool while the objects are selected, then tapping the selection with your finger or Apple Pencil to make the selection.

Note: If you are not seeing the Markup toolbar, click the Show Handwriting Tools button or Markup button. If the toolbar is minimized, click on its thumbnail.

2. Click the content you wish to evaluate after choosing it, then choose from one of the options below:
   - Cut, replicate, copy, or remove: Select a menu item.
   - Move the content by touching and holding it until it rises, then dragging it to a different spot.

Clear an error

Note: If you are not seeing the Markup toolbar, click the Show Handwriting Tools button or Markup button. If the toolbar is minimized, click on its thumbnail.

1. Select one of the subsequent actions after clicking the Eraser tool twice on the Markup toolbar:
2. Remove pixels: Select Pixel Eraser, then use your finger or an Apple Pencil to remove the error.
3. To remove an object, tap it with your finger or an Apple Pencil after selecting Object Eraser.
4. Utilize the Eraser tool once more and choose any of the pixel or object erasers to change between them.

Zoom in or out on iPad

Zoom

Via the Markup toolbar in a supported application (other than Notes), click the Annotate knob/button & then hit on the Magnifier.

Note: If you are not seeing the Markup toolbar, click the Show Handwriting Tools or Marker button. If the toolbar is minimized, click its thumbnail.

1. Try any of the subsequent to modify the characteristics of the magnifying glass:

- Change the zoom level by dragging the magnifying glasses green dot.
- Adjust the magnifying glasses size by dragging the blue dot on it.
- Move the magnifying glass: drag it.
- Modify the thickness of the magnifying glass outline: Tap the Shapes theme button, then pick an option.
- Change the border color around the magnifying glass: Pick a color with the color picker.
- Delete or make a copy of the magnifying glass: To delete or duplicate it, first press its outline.

2. To conceal the Markup toolbar after finishing, press the Show Handwriting Tools or Done button.

Accessing Wallet & Apple Pay quickly via the lock screen

You can access items on your tablet without having to unlock them if you have flight passes, coffee shop cards, or Apple Pay set up on the device:

1. Pressing the Home button twice will launch Apple Pay.
2. If you have multiple Apple Pay cards, swipe to choose the one you wish to use, or tap the bottom of the screen to choose a Wallet pass.

BOOK INDEX

116

Printed in Poland
by Amazon Fulfillment
Poland Sp. z o.o., Wrocław
24 November 2022

c8b2172c-55cb-478c-9f98-d77b016b542aR01